CAREER CATALYST:
Your Ultimate Guide to Landing Your Dream Job

Julian M. Fields

Table of Contents

Introduction

Have you ever felt stuck in your current job, dreaming of a more fulfilling and rewarding career? Perhaps you've sent out dozens of resumes, only to receive rejection after rejection. Or maybe you're unsure of what you even want to do with your life, feeling lost in a sea of endless options.

If this sounds familiar, you're not alone. The process of finding and landing your dream job can be overwhelming and intimidating. But it doesn't have to be that way.

That's why I've written this book, "Career Catalyst: Your Ultimate Guide to Landing Your Dream Job." With this guide, I aim to empower you with the tools and knowledge you need to take control of your career and achieve your professional goals.

Whether you're just starting out in your career or looking to make a change, this book will guide you through the process of self-discovery, job searching, and long-term career success. You'll learn how to identify your unique strengths and passions, build a targeted job search plan, and excel in your new role.

Don't settle for a job that leaves you unfulfilled. Let "Career Catalyst" be your guide to achieving the career of your dreams.

Chapter 1

Know Yourself

this is a phrase that has been attributed to many philosophers and thinkers throughout history, but its essence is always the same: it is a call to understand oneself, to delve deep into one's own thoughts, feelings, beliefs, values, and motivations in order to gain a greater sense of self-awareness.

Self-awareness is an important component of emotional intelligence and is a crucial factor in personal growth and development. It allows us to recognize our strengths and weaknesses, understand our own behavior and thought patterns, and make more informed decisions in our lives. When we know ourselves well, we are better equipped to set goals and pursue them, to communicate effectively with others, and to build healthy and fulfilling relationships.

Getting to know oneself is not always an easy task. It requires self-reflection, introspection, and a willingness to face uncomfortable truths about ourselves. It can involve examining past experiences and current behaviors to identify patterns and understand what motivates us. It can also involve exploring our values and beliefs to understand what drives our decision-making and shapes our worldview.

There are many tools and techniques that can help us in the process of self-discovery, including journaling, therapy, mindfulness practices, personality assessments, and feedback from others. Whatever methods we use, the goal is the same: to gain a greater understanding of ourselves and to use that knowledge to live more authentic, fulfilling lives.

On a philosophical level, it speaks to the idea that we as humans are complex beings with multifaceted identities, emotions, and experiences. It suggests that we should strive to understand our own unique perspectives and experiences so that we can better navigate the world around us.

On a practical level, knowing yourself can help you make better decisions, build stronger relationships, and achieve your goals. When you have a solid understanding of your own values, interests, and motivations, you are better able to prioritize what's important to you and pursue your passions. You can also identify areas where you may need to grow and develop in order to reach your full potential.

One way to get to know yourself better is through self-reflection. This can involve journaling, meditation, or simply taking time to think about your thoughts, feelings, and experiences. When you take the time to reflect on your experiences, you can identify patterns in your behavior and thought patterns that may be holding you back or causing you unnecessary stress.

Another way to get to know yourself better is through feedback from others. This can be both positive and negative feedback, and it can help you see yourself from a different perspective. By listening to what others have to say about you, you can gain insight into how your behavior affects those around you, and you can identify areas where you may need to make changes in order to improve your relationships and your overall well-being.

Self-awareness is also an important component of emotional intelligence. When you are aware of your own emotions and how they affect you, you are better able to regulate your own behavior and respond effectively to the emotions of others. This can lead to more positive and productive interactions with others, both in your personal and professional life.

Ultimately, the journey of "knowing yourself" is a lifelong one. It is not something that can be accomplished overnight or even in a few weeks or months. It requires ongoing self-reflection, a willingness to learn and grow, and a commitment to understanding your own unique perspective and experiences. But the rewards of this journey are many, and can lead to a more fulfilling and meaningful life.

Assessing your skills, strengths, and weaknesses

This is a crucial step in personal and professional development. It allows you to identify areas where you excel, as well as areas where you may need to improve. This information can help you make more informed decisions about your career, set realistic goals for yourself, and develop strategies to achieve them.

To assess your skills, strengths, and weaknesses, it can be helpful to start by taking an inventory of your abilities. This can involve making a list of the things you are good at, as well as the things you may struggle with. It can be helpful to ask yourself questions like:

What tasks do I enjoy doing?
What tasks do I find challenging?
What do others compliment me on?
What areas have I received negative feedback in the past?

Once you have identified your strengths and weaknesses, you can begin to think about how they relate to your personal and professional goals. For example, if you have identified strong communication skills as one of your strengths, you may consider pursuing a career in a field where communication is a key component. On the other hand, if you struggle with public speaking, you may need to work on developing those skills in order to advance in , and that it is normal to have areas where we may need more development. it is important to recognize that skills and strengths can be developed over time. For example, if you struggle with time management, you can work on developing better organizational habits or seeking out resources that can help you manage your time more effectively. Similarly, if you have identified strong problem-solving skills as one of your strengths, you can continue to develop those skills by seeking out new challenges and opportunities to problem-solve in your personal and professional life.

in addition is an essential aspect of personal and professional development that can enable you to achieve your goals and enhance your performance. In today's competitive environment, it is vital to understand your abilities, including the areas where you excel and those where you need to improve. This knowledge can help you pursue the right career path, set achievable goals, and take steps to develop the skills necessary for success.

When assessing your skills, strengths, and weaknesses, it is important to be honest with yourself. This process can be challenging as it requires a deep understanding of your capabilities and limitations. A useful way to approach this task is to take a skills inventory that highlights your areas of proficiency and those that require more work. For example, you may have exceptional interpersonal skills, but your time management skills may need improvement.

Once you have identified your skills and weaknesses, you can begin to develop strategies to address areas where you need to improve. This may include seeking additional training, finding a mentor who can offer guidance, or dedicating time to develop new skills through practice or courses. By developing an action plan that outlines your goals and the steps needed to achieve them, you can ensure that you are moving in the right direction.

Moreover, it is essential to understand your strengths and how they can benefit your personal and professional life. For instance, if you have excellent writing skills, you may consider a career in journalism or content creation. On the other hand, if you are good at problem-solving, you may pursue a career in engineering or science. Your strengths can also enable you to excel in your current role and increase your job satisfaction.

It is also important to assess your personal values and interests, as they can influence the choices you make in your career and life. For instance, if you value flexibility and work-life balance, you may prefer a remote work arrangement. Similarly, if you enjoy helping others, you may consider a career in healthcare or social work. By aligning your career choices with your values and interests, you can increase your motivation, job satisfaction, and overall wellbeing.

Additionally, feedback from others can be valuable in assessing your skills, strengths, and weaknesses. Seeking input from colleagues, supervisors, or mentors can help you gain a different perspective on your abilities, provide insights into areas where you can improve, and validate your strengths. Feedback can also help you identify blind spots, which are areas that you may not have considered or overlooked.

Assessing your skills, strengths, and weaknesses is a crucial step in personal and professional growth. It involves understanding your abilities, values, and interests to make informed decisions about your career and set achievable goals. By working to develop your skills and strengths while addressing areas where you need improvement, you can enhance your performance, increase job satisfaction, and lead a more fulfilling

Defining your career goals and values

This is an essential step in creating a fulfilling and successful professional life. Knowing what you want to achieve and what you stand for can help you make informed decisions and stay motivated towards your aspirations. In this article, we will explore the importance of career goals and values, and provide some tips on how to define them.

Career goals refer to the objectives you want to accomplish in your professional life. It could be a specific job position, a particular industry, a particular salary range, or a sense of fulfillment in your work. Setting clear and achievable career goals can help you stay focused and motivated, and provide a sense of direction in your professional life.

Values, on the other hand, are the principles and beliefs that guide your decision-making and behavior. They reflect your character and shape your interactions with others. Defining your values can help you identify what is important to you and align your career goals with your personal beliefs. Some common values include integrity, creativity, teamwork, respect, and growth.

To define your career goals and values, you can start by asking yourself some questions, such as:

What kind of work do I enjoy doing the most?
What skills and strengths do I have that can help me achieve my career goals?
What kind of impact do I want to make in my professional life?
What values are most important to me, and how can I reflect them in my work?

You can also seek feedback from mentors, colleagues, or career coaches to gain insights into your strengths and weaknesses, and identify areas where you can improve.

Defining your career goals involves identifying the specific objectives you want to achieve in your professional life. It could be a particular job position, a certain salary range, a specific industry, while long-term goals may take several years to accomplish. For example, a short-term goal could be to acquire a new skill or complete a project, while a long-term goal could be to become a team leader or start your own business.

Values, on the other hand, are the guiding principles that reflect your character and shape your interactions with others. Defining your values can help you identify what is important to you and align your career goals with your personal beliefs. Some common values include integrity, creativity, teamwork, respect, and growth.

To define your values, you can start by asking yourself what principles are most important to you, and how you can reflect them in your work. For example, if you value creativity, you may seek out a career in the arts, design, or innovation. If you value growth, you may focus on developing new skills and taking on challenging projects.

It is also important to regularly review and revise your career goals and values as you grow and evolve in your professional life. This can involve reassessing your priorities, identifying new opportunities, or adjusting your goals to align with your changing circumstances.

One effective way to stay on track with your career goals and values is to create a personal development plan. This involves setting specific goals, identifying the steps required to achieve them, and regularly reviewing your progress. You can also seek feedback from mentors, colleagues, or career coaches to gain insights into your strengths and weaknesses and identify areas where you can improve.

In conclusion, defining your career goals and values is an ongoing process that involves self-reflection, feedback, and action. By identifying what you want to achieve and what you stand for, you can create a more fulfilling and successful professional life that reflects your true self.

Identifying your personal brand and unique selling points

In today's competitive job market, identifying your personal brand and unique selling points is essential to standing out from the crowd and building a successful career. Your personal brand represents who you are, what you stand for, and the value you bring to the table. Your unique selling points, on the other hand, are the specific skills, strengths, and experiences that set you apart from others and make you an attractive candidate to potential employers.

Identifying your personal brand involves a deep understanding of your values, personality, and strengths. Your personal brand is not just about what you do, but how you do it and how you present yourself to the world. To define your personal brand, you can start by asking yourself questions like:

What are my core values, and how do they guide my behavior?
What are my strengths, and how can I leverage them in my career?

you can begin to develop a personal marketing plan that highlights your strengths and communicates your value to potential employers. This can involve creating a personal brand statement or elevator pitch that succinctly communicates your unique selling points and what you bring to the table.

To create a personal marketing plan, you can follow these steps:

- Identify your target audience: Who are the employers or industries you are targeting? What are their needs, goals, and pain points?

- Develop a value proposition: What is the unique value you bring to potential employers? What problems can you solve, or opportunities can you create?

- Build your brand: Develop a personal brand statement or elevator pitch that communicates your unique selling points and value proposition.

- Build your online presence: Establish a strong online presence through social media, personal websites, or blogs that showcase your skills and accomplishments.

- Network: Build relationships with colleagues, mentors, and industry professionals to expand your professional network and gain insights into potential job opportunities.

- Continuously learn and improve: Keep up-to-date with the latest industry trends and technologies, and invest in your professional development to continuously improve your skills and knowledge.

Identifying your personal brand and unique selling points is a crucial step towards building a successful and fulfilling career. By understanding your values, strengths, and unique perspective, you can create a personal marketing plan that communicates your value to potential employers and helps you stand out in a competitive job market. Remember that building a strong personal brand and unique selling points is an ongoing process that requires self-reflection, feedback, and action.

Developing a clear career narrative

This is essential for effectively communicating your career goals, experiences, and achievements to potential employers or colleagues. A career narrative is essentially your personal story of your professional journey, and it can be a powerful tool for demonstrating your skills, strengths, and potential for future success.

A clear career narrative should be concise, compelling, and focused on the key themes or accomplishments that best represent your career journey. It should highlight your core values, goals, and motivations, and showcase how your experiences. When crafting your career narrative, it is important to keep in mind the context of your audience. Your narrative should be tailored to the needs and interests of the person or group you are communicating with. This may involve highlighting specific skills or achievements that are relevant to the job or industry, or focusing on specific challenges you have overcome that demonstrate your ability to handle difficult situations.

A clear career narrative can be used in a variety of settings, including job interviews, networking events, or professional bios. It can help you make a strong first impression, demonstrate your unique value to potential employers or colleagues, and stand out in a competitive job market.

Here are some additional details on developing a clear career narrative:

- Reflect on your career journey: When reflecting on your career journey, it is important to consider your past experiences, achievements, and challenges. This can involve looking back at previous jobs, internships, or volunteer work, and identifying the skills and knowledge you have gained from those experiences. You can also think about key moments or milestones in your career that have helped shape your goals and values.

- Identify key themes and accomplishments: Once you have reflected on your career journey, you can start identifying key themes and accomplishments that best represent your story. These may include specific skills or experiences that you have developed over time, or achievements that demonstrate your ability to handle challenging situations. It is important to focus on the themes and accomplishments that are most relevant to your current or future career goals.

- Develop a story arc: A story arc is a narrative structure that involves identifying a clear beginning, middle, and end to your career story. The beginning should establish your goals and motivations, the middle should showcase the key experiences and accomplishments that have helped you grow and develop, and the end should demonstrate your current or future career goals. A strong story arc can help ensure that your career narrative is cohesive and easy to follow.

- Craft a compelling narrative: Crafting a compelling narrative involves communicating your career goals, experiences, and achievements in a clear and concise way. It is important to focus on the most relevant information and to use concrete examples to illustrate your points. Your narrative should also highlight your unique strengths and values, and demonstrate how these can help you succeed in your current or future career.

- Practice and refine: Practicing and refining your career narrative is important for ensuring that it is clear, concise, and impactful. You can practice by telling your story to friends, mentors, or colleagues, and using their feedback to improve your narrative. It is also important to update and refine your narrative as your career evolves, and to tailor it to the needs and interests of your audience.

Chapter 2

Strategize Your Job Search

This is an essential step in finding a job that is a good fit for your skills, values, and career goals. By taking a strategic approach to your job search, you can save time and effort, and increase your chances of finding a job that meets your needs.

Here are some steps to help you strategize your job search:

- Clarify your goals and priorities: Before you begin your job search, take time to clarify your career goals and priorities. This can involve identifying the type of job you want, the industry you want to work in, and the skills and experience you want to gain. You should also consider your personal and financial goals, and how they align with your career goals.

- Research potential employers: Once you have clarified your goals and priorities, you can start researching potential employers. This can involve looking at job postings, reading company profiles, and networking with professionals in your desired industry. By researching potential employers, you can gain a better understanding of their values, culture, and hiring practices.

- Develop a targeted resume and cover letter: A targeted resume and cover letter can help you stand out from other job candidates. Your resume should be tailored to the specific job you are applying for, and should highlight your relevant skills and experience. Your cover letter should explain why you are interested in the job and how you can contribute to the company.

- Network: Networking is a key part of any job search. You can network by attending industry events, reaching out to professionals in your desired field, and connecting with alumni from your school. By networking, you can gain valuable insights into the job market, and potentially uncover job opportunities that are not posted online.

- Prepare for interviews: Once you have applied for a job, you may be called for an interview. It is important to prepare for interviews by researching the company, practicing common interview questions, and preparing examples of your past experience that demonstrate your skills and abilities.

- Evaluate job offers: If you are offered a job, take time to evaluate the offer to ensure it aligns with your career goals and priorities. This may involve considering factors such as salary, benefits, company culture, and potential for growth and development.

By taking a strategic approach to your job search, you can save time and effort, and increase your chances of finding a job that is a good fit for your skills, values, and career goals. Remember to stay organized, stay focused on your goals, and be persistent in your search. With time and effort, you can find a job that is a perfect fit for you.

Understanding the current job market and industry trends

Understanding the current job market and industry trends is essential for job seekers, employees, and employers to make informed decisions about career choices and business strategies. It involves gaining insights into the current state of the economy, labor market, and industry-specific trends that affect employment opportunities, skill demands, and job requirements.

To understand the job market, it's important to look at the overall economic conditions, such as GDP growth, inflation, and interest rates. These factors can impact the job market by affecting business growth and consumer spending. Additionally, it's important to understand the demographic shifts in the workforce, such as age, gender, and ethnic diversity, as these can also impact employment opportunities.

Industry trends refer to the changes, developments, and innovations in a specific field or sector. To understand these trends, one should stay updated with the latest news, research reports, and expert opinions in the industry. For example, in the technology sector, trends such as artificial intelligence, big data, and the Internet of Things (IoT) are driving the demand for new skills and competencies, including programming, data analytics, and cybersecurity.

Understanding the current job market and industry trends can help job seekers identify areas of growth and opportunity in their field, and adapt their skills and qualifications accordingly. Employers can also use this information to anticipate changes in their industry and adjust their hiring and training strategies to stay competitive.

To gain a better understanding of the job market, it's important to analyze employment data, including the unemployment rate, job growth, and wages. This data can provide insights into which industries and job roles are in demand, and which ones are facing challenges. Additionally, it's important to consider the effects of the COVID-19 pandemic, which has had a significant impact on the global job market. Many industries have faced disruption or decline, while others have experienced growth and expansion due to changes in consumer behavior and demand. To gain a better understanding of the job market, it's important to analyze employment data, including the unemployment rate, job growth, and wages. This data can provide insights into which industries and job roles are in demand, and which ones are facing challenges.

To stay updated on industry trends, there are several sources of information that can be helpful. These include industry associations, trade publications, and market research firms. These sources can provide information on emerging technologies, changing consumer preferences, and shifts in the competitive landscape. It's also important to network with industry professionals, attend industry events, and participate in online forums and discussions to gain insights and knowledge from peers and experts.

In addition to understanding the broader economic and industry trends, it's also important to assess your own skills and qualifications in relation to the job market. This can involve identifying in-demand skills and competencies, such as digital skills, communication skills, and critical thinking, and evaluating whether you possess these skills or need to acquire them through training or education.

Overall, understanding the current job market and industry trends is an ongoing process that requires continuous learning and adaptation. By staying informed and proactive, job seekers and employers can make informed decisions and take advantage of opportunities in the job market.

Networking effectively online and offline

This is an essential component of personal and professional development. Building connections with like-minded individuals can help you expand your horizons, learn from others, and open doors to new opportunities. However, networking can seem daunting at first, particularly if you're not naturally outgoing or don't have a lot of experience with socializing. Here are some additional tips to help you network effectively in both realms:

Networking Online:

- Utilize social media: Social media platforms like LinkedIn, Twitter, and Facebook are great tools for networking with professionals in your industry. You can search for groups, forums, or chats that pertain to your interests and connect with other people in the group. Make sure your profiles are up-to-date and well-crafted to reflect your expertise and experience.

- Be authentic: When reaching out to people online, always strive to be genuine and professional. Avoid coming across as pushy or insincere, and instead, focus on building relationships by taking a genuine interest in others and their work.

- Participate in online communities: Engage with others by commenting, sharing and posting relevant content. You can join industry groups or participate in webinars or online events to learn more about your field.

Networking Offline:

- Attend industry events: Conferences, trade shows, and seminars are excellent opportunities to meet other professionals in your field. These events often have networking receptions or other opportunities to connect with others in a more relaxed setting. Prepare in advance by researching speakers or attendees and creating a list of individuals you want to connect with.

- Join local business groups: Rotary clubs, Chambers of Commerce, and other local organizations can help you connect with other professionals in your area. These groups often have regular meetings or events where you can get to know other members and learn about local businesses.
- Volunteer: Nonprofits and community organizations are great places to meet people who share your interests and passions. You can gain valuable experience while networking and building relationships with others.
- Attend social events: Mixers, happy hours, and other events provide opportunities to meet new people and

socialize in a more relaxed setting. Make sure you bring your business cards or other contact information so you can exchange them with others.

No matter where you're networking, it's important to remember to be authentic, respectful and genuine in your interactions. Building strong relationships takes time, effort, and patience, but the benefits can be substantial, both personally and professionally. Remember to follow up with people after meeting them and stay in touch with those you have connected with. By putting yourself out there, taking initiative and being open to learning and growing, you can create a network of valuable connections that will support you in your personal and professional journey.

Preparing for job interviews and negotiations

Preparing for job interviews and negotiations is a critical step in securing a job offer that aligns with your career goals and aspirations. Job interviews give you an opportunity to showcase your skills and experience, while negotiations help you reach a mutually beneficial agreement on your compensation and other benefits. The process can be nerve-wracking, especially if you are new to job searching or have not interviewed or negotiated in a while. However, adequate preparation can help you overcome your anxieties and present yourself in the best possible light.

One of the most important aspects of preparing for job interviews and negotiations is researching the company. You need to have a clear understanding of the organization's history, culture, mission, and values. Look up the company website and social media pages, and read news articles and press releases to get a sense of the company's recent developments and future plans. Also, try to find out who will be conducting the interview, their job title, and their areas of responsibility. This will help you tailor your responses to the interviewer's interests and demonstrate your fit for the company.

Another crucial step in preparing for job interviews and negotiations is preparing your responses. Start by reviewing the job description and identifying the most important qualifications and responsibilities. Then, brainstorm examples from your work experience that demonstrate your ability to meet these qualifications and perform the duties effectively. Practice your responses out loud, ideally in front of a mirror or with a friend or mentor. This will help you refine your delivery, increase your confidence, and identify areas where you need to improve.

In addition to preparing your responses, it is essential to prepare questions to ask the interviewer. This shows your interest in the position and the company and helps you determine if the role is a good fit for you. Think about questions that will help you understand the company's culture, expectations, and opportunities for growth. For example, you could ask about the company's most significant challenges or successes, the team's composition, the performance metrics for the position, or the opportunities for continuing education and professional development.

Dressing appropriately is another important aspect of preparing for job interviews and negotiations. Dressing professionally conveys your respect for the company and the interviewer and helps you feel more confident and polished. Choose an outfit that is clean, pressed, and fits well. Make sure your accessories and grooming are appropriate and not distracting. If you are not sure what to wear, you can always ask the recruiter or hiring manager for guidance.

Practice your body language and communication skills to make a positive impression during the interview or negotiation. Start by practicing confident body language, such as sitting up straight, making eye contact, and smiling. These nonverbal cues convey your interest and enthusiasm for the position. Also, make sure you speak clearly, concisely, and confidently, and listen actively to the interviewer's questions and comments. Show that you are engaged in the conversation by nodding, making affirmative statements, and asking follow-up questions.

When it comes to negotiating salary or other benefits, it is essential to know your worth and be prepared to advocate for yourself. Research the industry standards and the company's compensation structure to determine what is fair and reasonable for your experience and qualifications. Also, consider your personal circumstances, such as your financial obligations, career aspirations, and lifestyle goals. When you present your counteroffer, be specific, polite, and respectful. Avoid making ultimatums or appearing confrontational, as this can damage the relationship and reduce the likelihood of a positive outcome.

Chapter 3

Excel in Your Career

This requires a combination of hard work, dedication, and strategic thinking. Whether you are just starting your career or are a seasoned professional, there are several key principles you can follow to achieve success and satisfaction in your work.

- Set clear goals: The first step in excelling in your career is to define what you want to achieve. This means setting clear and achievable goals for your career path. Consider where you want to be in five or ten years, what skills you need to develop, and what types of experiences you need to gain. Write down your goals and create an action plan to achieve them. Make sure to review and adjust your goals regularly to ensure you stay on track.

- Invest in your education: Continuous learning is crucial for success in today's rapidly changing job market. Take courses, attend workshops, and seek out mentorship opportunities to help you develop the skills you need to excel in your field. Consider pursuing advanced degrees or certifications to boost your credentials and increase your marketability.

- Build a strong network: A strong professional network is essential for career success. Attend industry events, join professional organizations, and connect with colleagues on social media to expand your circle of contacts. Stay in touch with your network and offer support and help when you can. Your network can be a valuable source of career advice, job leads, and professional development opportunities.

- Develop a strong work ethic: Successful professionals are known for their strong work ethic. This means being punctual, dependable, and reliable. Always meet or exceed expectations, take initiative, and be a team player. Take on additional responsibilities and seek out opportunities to contribute to your organization's success.

- Focus on your strengths: To excel in your career, it's important to focus on your strengths and build upon them. Identify your unique talents and skills, and seek out opportunities to use them in your work. Look for ways to develop new skills that complement your existing strengths. This will help you become a valuable asset to your organization and stand out from your peers.

- Communicate effectively: Effective communication is a key skill for career success. This means listening actively, expressing yourself clearly and confidently, and being able to adapt your communication style to different situations and audiences. Focus on building strong relationships with your colleagues and stakeholders by communicating openly and honestly.

- Take calculated risks: Taking calculated risks can help you grow in your career. This means stepping out of your comfort zone and trying new things that can help you learn and grow. Seek out challenging assignments, ask for feedback, and embrace new opportunities. Taking calculated risks can help you build confidence, gain new skills, and demonstrate your value to your organization.

Making a smooth transition into your new role

This refers to the process of shifting from your old position to a new one in a seamless and efficient way. This involves a deliberate and strategic plan to integrate yourself into the new role and the new team, while also gradually disengaging from your previous responsibilities.

The following are some steps that can help you make a smooth transition into your new role:

- Learn as much as you can about the new role: Before starting your new job, it is important to learn about your new role and the responsibilities that come with it. You can do this by reviewing the job description, asking your supervisor or colleagues questions, and doing research on the company and industry.

- Build relationships with your new colleagues: Building relationships with your new colleagues is key to a smooth transition. Take time to get to know your coworkers, their roles, and their interests. This will help you understand how you can best work together and support one another.

- Understand the company culture: Each company has its own unique culture, and it's important to understand this to ensure a smooth transition. Pay attention to how your coworkers interact with one another, what is valued in the workplace, and the company's mission and values.

Communicate with your supervisor: Your supervisor can be a valuable resource during your transition. Communicate with them regularly, ask for feedback, and set goals for yourself to ensure you are meeting expectations.

- Be patient and flexible: Remember that it takes time to adjust to a new role. Be patient with yourself and be open to making changes as you learn and grow in your new position.

Additionally, building strong relationships with your new colleagues is a key aspect of making a smooth transition. You can do this by getting to know them and their roles, learning about their interests, and finding common ground. This will help you to build trust and understanding with your coworkers, which is important for effective collaboration and a positive work environment.

Understanding the company culture is also crucial for making a successful transition. Each company has its own unique culture, which influences how people communicate and work together. By understanding the company culture, you can adapt your communication style, work effectively with your colleagues, and better navigate any potential conflicts that may arise.

Communicating with your supervisor is another important step in making a smooth transition. Your supervisor can provide you with valuable feedback and guidance to help you succeed in your new role. Be sure to set goals with your supervisor to ensure that you are meeting expectations and to identify areas for growth and development.

Building strong relationships with colleagues and supervisors

One important aspect of building strong relationships with colleagues and supervisors is establishing rapport. This means taking the time to get to know your colleagues and supervisors on a personal level, beyond just the work that you do. This can involve sharing personal stories, interests, and hobbies, and finding common ground with your colleagues and supervisors. By establishing rapport, you can build a stronger connection with your colleagues and supervisors and create a more positive and enjoyable work environment.

Another way to build strong relationships with colleagues and supervisors is to show appreciation for their contributions. This can be as simple as saying "thank you" when someone helps you out or acknowledging a job well done. When you show appreciation for your colleagues and supervisors, they are more likely to feel valued and motivated to continue doing good work.

Building strong relationships with colleagues and supervisors also involves being adaptable and flexible. In a work environment, things can change quickly, and it's important to be able to adapt to new situations and take on new responsibilities. By being flexible, you can demonstrate that you are a team player and that you are willing to go above and beyond to help your colleagues and supervisors achieve their goals.

Taking initiative is another important aspect of building strong relationships with colleagues and supervisors. This means taking the lead in establishing relationships, offering to help out in areas where you have skills or knowledge, and seeking out opportunities to learn and grow. By taking initiative, you can demonstrate that you are committed to building strong relationships and contributing to the success of your team. It is also important to be proactive in building strong relationships with colleagues and supervisors. This means taking the initiative to schedule meetings or social events outside of work to get to know your colleagues and supervisors better. You can also take the initiative to offer your help or expertise in areas where you have skills or knowledge.

Establishing rapport is an essential part of building strong relationships with colleagues and supervisors. This means taking the time to get to know your colleagues and supervisors on a personal level. It involves having conversations that go beyond just work-related topics, sharing personal stories, interests, and hobbies, and finding common ground with your colleagues and supervisors. This can help to create a more positive and enjoyable work environment, as well as foster a sense of camaraderie and trust.

Showing appreciation is another important aspect of building strong relationships with colleagues and supervisors. This can involve expressing gratitude for someone's help or support, acknowledging a job well done, or simply saying "thank you" for something someone has done. By showing appreciation, you can make your colleagues and supervisors feel valued and motivated to continue doing good work.

Being adaptable and flexible is also crucial when it comes to building strong relationships with colleagues and supervisors. In any workplace, things can change quickly, and it's important to be able to adapt to new situations and take on new responsibilities. By being flexible, you can demonstrate that you are a team player and that you are willing to go above and beyond to help your colleagues and supervisors achieve their goals. This can lead to a greater sense of trust and respect from your colleagues and supervisors. Another important aspect of building strong relationships with colleagues and supervisors is managing conflicts effectively. In any workplace, conflicts can arise, and it's important to address them promptly and constructively. This involves listening to all parties involved, seeking to understand their perspectives, and working together to find a resolution that is acceptable to everyone.

Finally, building strong relationships with colleagues and supervisors involves demonstrating a commitment to personal and professional growth. This means seeking out opportunities to learn new skills, taking on challenging projects, and asking for feedback from your colleagues and supervisors. When you show a commitment to personal and professional growth, you demonstrate that you are a valuable asset to your team and that you are willing to put in the effort to improve yourself and the work that you do.

Developing new skills and pursuing professional development opportunities

Developing new skills and pursuing professional development opportunities are important for staying relevant and competitive in the workplace. Here are some more details:

- Identifying the skills you need: Before you start pursuing new skills, it's important to identify the skills that you need for your current or future job. You can do this by reviewing job descriptions, talking to colleagues and mentors, and researching industry trends.

- Choosing the right development opportunities: Once you have identified the skills you need, you can look for professional development opportunities that will help you acquire those skills. This can include attending conferences, workshops, and webinars, taking online courses or training programs, and pursuing advanced degrees.

- Setting goals: It's important to set specific and measurable goals for your professional development. This can help you stay motivated and focused, and ensure that you are making progress towards your objectives.

- Making time for learning: Learning new skills takes time and effort, so it's important to make time for it in your schedule. This can include dedicating a certain amount of time each day or week to learning, or taking time off from work to attend conferences or training programs.

- Networking: Networking can be a valuable way to learn about new opportunities and connect with other professionals in your field. You can network by attending industry events, joining professional organizations, and reaching out to colleagues and mentors.

- Applying your new skills: Finally, it's important to apply your new skills in your work to demonstrate their value to your employer and continue to improve your performance. This can also help you build a portfolio of work that showcases your abilities to potential employers.

- Emphasizing soft skills: In addition to technical or hard skills, soft skills like communication, leadership, and problem-solving are highly valued by employers. You can develop these skills by seeking out training opportunities, practicing effective communication, and taking on leadership roles in your workplace.

- Seeking feedback: Getting feedback from colleagues, mentors, and supervisors can help you identify areas for improvement and focus your professional development efforts. Don't be afraid to ask for feedback and be open to constructive criticism.

- Taking advantage of employer resources: Some employers offer professional development resources like training programs, conferences, or tuition reimbursement. Take advantage of these resources to enhance your skills and demonstrate your commitment to your career.

- Pursuing diverse learning opportunities: Don't limit yourself to one type of learning opportunity. Try a variety of methods like online courses, mentoring, job shadowing, or volunteering to gain exposure to different experiences and perspectives.

- Keeping up with industry trends: To stay relevant and competitive in your field, it's important to keep up with industry trends and emerging technologies. You can do this by reading industry publications, attending conferences, and following thought leaders in your field.

Conclusion

Congratulations! You've reached the end of "Career Catalyst: Your Ultimate Guide to Landing Your Dream Job." I hope that this guide has provided you with the inspiration and knowledge you need to take your career to the next level. Throughout the book, we've covered a wide range of topics, including self-assessment, job search strategies, and long-term career success. But more than that, we've explored the mindset and values that are necessary to truly excel in your career.

Landing your dream job is not a one-time event. It requires ongoing self-reflection, learning, and growth. It requires the courage to take risks and the persistence to keep pushing forward even in the face of setbacks.But with the knowledge and strategies outlined in this guide, you have the power to take control of your career and create the future you've always wanted. You now have a clear understanding of your strengths, values, and passions, and know how to articulate your personal brand to potential employers. You also know how to build a targeted job search plan that maximizes your chances of landing your dream job, whether that involves networking, creating a strong resume and cover letter, or acing the job interview.

But landing your dream job is just the first step. In order to truly excel in your career, you'll need to continue to grow and develop your skills, pursue new opportunities, and build strong relationships with colleagues and mentors.

Remember, success in your career is not just about what you achieve, but how you achieve it. It's about staying true to your values and passions, and making a positive impact in the lives of those around you.

So as you move forward on your journey, keep these principles in mind. Don't be afraid to take risks and pursue your passions, but always do so with integrity and authenticity. Build strong relationships with colleagues and mentors, and continue to seek out opportunities for growth and development. With these principles in mind, there is no limit to what you can achieve. Thank you for taking the time to read "Career Catalyst." I wish you all the best on your journey to success and fulfillment in your career.

www.ingramcontent.com/pod-product-compliance
Lightning Source LLC
Chambersburg PA
CBHW071141220526
45467CB00015B/1683